CW01022257

Say Something Happened

A play

Alan Bennett

Samuel French—London
New York-Toronto-Hollywood

Please see page iv for further copyright information

SAY SOMETHING HAPPENED

First presented on television by BBC2 on 17th December 1982 with the following cast:

Mam   Thora Hird
Dad   Hugh Lloyd
June Potter   Julie Walters

Produced by Innes Lloyd
Directed by Giles Foster
Designed by Austin Ruddy
Music by George Fenton

SAY SOMETHING HAPPENED

The hall and living-room of a semi-detached house. Day

A couple in their sixties are sitting there, the man in an easy chair, the woman gazing out of the window. Pause

Mam More leaves coming down. (*Pause*) Straight on to our path. (*Pause*) I could be in and out all day. (*Pause*) It's not right. It's her tree, yet somehow they're our leaves.

Dad I might get down the atlas in a minute. (*Pause*) Try and spot Helsinki.

Mam I'm just wondering if I ought to wash one or two stockings.

Dad gets up to get the atlas

Don't upset. I've just this minute sat down. (*Pause*) I shouldn't know where to look.

Dad Helsinki. Oh yes. It's the capital of Finland. It was a station on the little wireless we had when we were first married. Hilversum. Helsinki. Droitwich. No end of different places.

Mam All radio this that and the other now.

Dad It won't be so warm. Getting on for the Arctic Circle.

Mam It's to be hoped she takes them little bootee things we bought her. They'll be just what the doctor ordered in the Arctic Circle.

Dad is turning over the pages of the atlas

Dad It can't be so far off Russia.

Mam (*alarmed*) Russia?

Dad She's a sensible girl. Russia won't worry our Margaret. (*He reads out the statistics from the atlas*) "Helsinki. Seaport and capital city of Finland. Population two-point-seven million. Chief industries: carpets, sugar, paper-making ——

The doorchimes go

— fisheries."

Mam I hope this isn't next door. (*She stands up and looks out of the window*) It's a young woman.

Dad What sort of a young woman? (*He gets up*)

Mam Educated. Got a briefcase. You go. Only, Dad …

Dad is going out into the hall. He pauses

Put the chain on.

In the hall Dad puts the chain on and opens the door

We don't see the young woman on the other side and the following is spoken through the open crack of the door

Dad Hallo.

June (*off*) Mr Rhodes?

Dad Yes.

June (*off*) June Potter. I'm from the council. The Social Services Department.

Dad Yes?

June (*off*) You had a leaflet.

Dad What leaflet?

June (*off*) You should have had a leaflet. Put through.

Dad (*calling*) Mam. Have we had a leaflet?

Mam comes out into the hall

Mam What about?

June (*off*) The register. Old people in the council area.

Mam (*mouthing to Dad*) I threw it away. (*Pause*) We're not council tenants. You've got mistaken.

June (*off*) Hullo?

Dad Yes?

June (*off*) Rhodes, Arthur. Rhodes, Elizabeth Mary.

Dad Well?

June (*off*) It's not confined to council tenants. It's all senior citizens in the council area. We have you down as pensioners.

Mam (*mouthing*) Ask her for her card.

Dad She looks right enough.

Mam She should have a card. There was a woman at Bramley gagged with her own tights, and they said they were gasmen.

Suddenly the card is held round the door and moved up and down. Dad takes it and hands it to Mam. He then unchains the door

It is June Potter, a girl in her early twenties wearing a cape

Does this reckon to be you? June Potter?

June Yes.

Mam The hair's different.

June I wasn't in Social Services then. I was Transport. I had it frizzed out. They tend to be more relaxed in Social Services.

Mam It's not the same colour.

June I'd just got back from Torquay.

Dad It is her.

June I might have had it dyed, then. I can't remember.

Mam Dyed?

June A cream rinse.

Mam I thought you said you worked for the council. My uncle worked for the council, and you'd never see him without a collar and tie.

Dad They all dye their hair nowadays. Lads. Everybody.

Mam He wore a suit every day of his life did my uncle.

June Social Services they make us wear what we like.

Mam That's one of them poncho affairs, isn't it?

Dad Well, I've seen Princess Anne in one of them.

Mam Not since she got married.
June It's just a matter of one or two questions.
Dad Fetch her inside. She's only young.
Mam You keep saying that. Youth's no guarantee nowadays.
There was a woman attacked in the Grasmeres and it left her a
vegetable. Wipe your feet.

June comes in and they go through into the living-room

(*Entering the room*) If you want to come waltzing into people's
houses you ought to get yourself a little costume. You'd look
heaps better in a two-piece, and you'd find people much more
forthcoming. She wants to take a leaf out of our Margaret's book.
Dad They can't all be like our Margaret.
Mam That's a change, coming from you. Sit down. Do you want
some tea?

June nods

Mam goes out to the kitchen

(*Off*) Sending out questionnaires. They want to do something
about public toilets. Stuff written up on walls. Them little rings
from beer cans you see lying about everywhere — never mind
questionnaires.

*Dad has been embarrassed by all this, and is more anxious to put
June at her ease*

Dad She's hyper-careful is Mam.
June No, full marks. There are very few people your age know how
to answer the door. I wish I could show her to Mr Farquarson. At
night I walk down the middle of the road.

Pause

Dad I like those poncho things, personally.

June Mr Farquarson tells us not to dress up. Otherwise we get into an "us" and "them" situation. (*Pause*) These are in fact old ski pants.

Dad nods. Pause

Dad Not them jogging things?
June No.

Pause

Dad Not a jogger?
June No fear. (*Pause*) Thin enough!

June prepares her interviewing kit — clipboard, form, pencil — very methodically

Dad What's it to do with, this questionnaire?
June No. (*Reading from her notebook as if talking to a child*) "Where possible, interviewer should endeavour to see all members of the household together." I've never done this before, so I have to stick to the book of words. (*Pause*) You know ... structured.
Dad Don't want telling two different tales. (*Pause*) Tip-top job, now, working for the Council.
June They took me on to do discs. Controlled parking.
Dad }
June } (*together*) Transport.
June Then the inevitable happened. Computers. I went and saw Mr Stringfellow and he said, "My advice to you, June, is to do a bit of a sideways jump and get yourself into the S.S." Social Services.
Dad We don't have a parking problem. We don't have a car.
June I prefer working with people to cars. They're more unpredictable but they're more rewarding. With me people come first. Old people specifically. Older people.

Pause

Dad They are a problem.
June Yes.
Dad Where to put them. They have to be put somewhere.

Pause

June Old people?
Dad Cars. I've often thought, if we had one I could put one of those carport affairs inside the front gate. There's room.
June As I see it, young people have a lot to give old people, and old people have a lot to give young people. You know … *caring*.
Dad I agree. With a car our daughter can run us to Ilkley. Or Knaresborough. Will you be motorized?
June I've got my trusty moped, only the clutch has packed in, so I'm sampling public transport.
Dad Your parents'll have a car?
June Split up.
Dad Oh. (*Pause*) That's on the up and up.
June What?
Dad Divorce.

Mam returns with the tea things

Mam How do you like your tea? We like ours strong.
June Weak, please. No milk.
Mam No milk?
June No milk.
Mam Whatever for?
Dad Because that's how she likes it.
June I generally have lemon. I don't want lemon but that's what I have.
Dad I've seen our Margaret have lemon.
Mam Only in a café. We haven't got any lemon.
Dad We've got one of those plastic squirters. Lemon juice.
June That'll do.

Dad gets up to go into the kitchen

Mam And Dad. Some little plates.

He goes

All that's come in now. Lemon in your tea. Yogurt. Carrying babies on your back. We weren't brought up to any of that. I was thought a bit revolutionary for having prunes.

Dad returns with the plastic lemon and plates

Not them plates, Dad. The *side*plates.

She goes out

Dad You're not bothered about sideplates? (*Calling*) She's not bothered about sideplates.
Mam (*off, calling from the kitchen*) She wants a scone.
June (*to Dad*) I don't want anything to eat.
Dad (*calling*) She doesn't want anything to eat.

Mam returns with the sideplates

Mam You'll have a scone?
June No. I'm on a diet. I get migraine.
Mam From scones?
June It's a special-type non-gluten diet. They've only just pin-pointed it. I haven't to have flour.
Dad It's a terrible scourge, migraine. Our daughter gets migraine.
Mam Not from scones. It's chocolate with her. I've never heard of anyone getting headaches from scones.
Dad Look at me. I can't do with tomatoes.
Mam That's your bowels.
Dad (*embarrassed*) Mam.
Mam (*poised with the plastic lemon*) One squirt or two squirts?
Dad Let her squirt it herself.
June One please.

Mam squirts it

Can we start? This is the leaflet you should have had and I will read it to you.

Dad Mam threw it away.

Mam I didn't throw it away. It got thrown away.

June (*reading*) "In recent months there have been one or two mishaps involving old people, senior citizens who have become isolated within the community. Some genuine tragedies have occurred. Accordingly your council has decided to compile a register of all persons of pensionable age within the council area. The establishment of such a register will ——"

Mam Hypothermia.

June stops

Is that it? Hypothermia? Not us. (*She points*) We've got a Dimplex. Background heating.

Dad Plus a fire.

Mam Dimplex and a fire.

Dad For company.

Mam The fire's company. The Dimplex isn't company.

Dad I didn't say the Dimplex was company.

June Anyway. That takes care of question seven: source of heating. Any heating in the bedroom?

Mam Him.

Dad Mam.

Mam This is old people. It's not us. You want Miss Venables over the road. She has a pacemaker and her friend comes in from Bramley.

June has been told to expect such a reaction, and covertly consults her notebook

June Hang on ... "the refusal to recognize the approach of old age and the possibility of infirmity is entirely natural ... and in its way commendable." That was Mr Farquarson, last week. (*She laughs* *in a stilted way)* You are as old as you feel. But let me sketch out a possible scenario. You're not feeling too clever; you're in bed. Mr Rhodes goes to fetch the milk, it's slippy and bang, that's his hip gone. Hearing a shout you get up, go downstairs and try shifting him. You promptly have a dizzy do and bang, that's two of you lying on the path in sub-zero temperatures. You won't last long.

Pause

Mam The point is, we don't want roping in for any get-togethers.

Dad That's it. They put you on a register, next minute you're sitting round banging a tambourine.

June *(reading again)* No. "When your council has compiled the register a number of Old People's Wardens will be appointed, whose job it will be to keep track of all old people in the area, particularly those who are 'at risk'."

Mam Oh. It's "at risk" is it? That's something else that's come in, "at risk". There never used to be that, did there, "at risk". It's all "at risk" now. Battered babies, battered wives ... are you sure you won't have a scone?

June No.

Dad You do read some shocking stories. There was an old lass at Moortown got eaten by her own alsatian.

Mam Her own silly fault. I wouldn't have an alsatian. They always revert. We don't want pestering to go to bingo. Joining in. That's what choked us off with church.

June This isn't bingo, Mrs Rhodes. This is survival.

Pause

Dad We aren't good mixers, that's the trouble.

Mam You're not. I am. I used to be a right good mixer.

Dad You never were.

Mam I went to the Fellowship.

Dad When they lassooed you first. We're neither of us anything in the mixing line. We were when we were first married but you lose the knack.

June makes a note

Mam What is it you're writing down?
June Nothing.
Mam What did we say?
June Nothing.

There is a silence. June doodles, embarrassed, on her pad, then talks while she's doodling

    Mr Farquarson said that th : .urvey would be a chance for us to do a little *ad hoc* assessment. Part of our training. You know, fieldwork. Only I'm not supposed to tell you that.
Mam We're guinea pigs.
Dad She has to learn.
Mam Not on us she doesn't.
June I was just noting you both seem very alert mentally.
Dad There you are.
Mam Mentally?
June And you quarrel. That's another good sign.
Mam We never do. We never have a wrong word.
June You don't agree always. You *spar*. Look on it as a sign of life. Vitality. On a scale of one to ten you've got eight.
Mam Why not ten?
June Nobody gets ten. The Queen Mother wouldn't get ten. This is the joy of the job for me. I did surveys in Transport … traffic projections, long haul or short haul, purpose of trip … only there was no feedback. The beauty of this is … it's people. This is what they call interaction.

A long pause with interaction notably absent

    What were we saying?

Mam won't speak

    You were talking about church. How you used to go to church.

Dad They got this new young vicar.

Mam (*reluctantly*) It was the singing we liked.

Dad He kept wanting these discussions. Forums. Race. Religion. Current affairs. We stopped going.

June That's a pity.

Mam Why, do you go to church?

June No.

Dad That's with you being educated. God's always the first casualty. One time he had us all talking about Buddha. Well Mam doesn't know anything about Buddha. And I don't know anything about Buddha. And the Third World.

Mam I don't even know where that is. We just haven't been educated.

Dad No dog collar. Always wore civvies. It's as if they're ashamed of it.

Mam Last time we went to church, in the middle of the service he suddenly gets up and says, "Now, I want you all to shake hands with the person on either side of you." Well Dad was all right because he was sat on the aisle, so he'd only to shake hands with me, but I got a right common woman in a leopardskin coat. I'd never seen her before in my life.

June But that's good, isn't it?

Mam Yes, I can see you're in the same brigade.

June Isolation, that's the bugbear.

Mam We don't mind a bit of isolation. It's the other *we* don't like. He had a couple kissing on the front of the parish magazine. Christian Love. I'd prefer little kiddies with rice bowls, I would.

Dad I don't see that God is to do with mixing. Too much God, and it puts the tin hat on it.

Mam What about you, do you mix?

June I tend to run across people at work. I'm not at risk. I'm not old.

Mam Old, old. There's risks with youth. You might commit suicide. That's snowballed.

Dad Mam.

Mam Well. How old are your parents?

Dad Nay, they've split up, haven't they?

Mam Split up? Are you married?

June No.

Mam Where do you live?

June Kirkstall.

Mam They've knocked most of it down. Is it a flat?

June A bedsitter.

Mam A bedsitter? Child of a broken home, living in a bedsitter in one of these inner city areas: you're the one that's at risk. You want to get *yourself* on a register. Coming round telling us. Isolated. We like being isolated. We're like that. It's the same as the radio now, every programme you turn on, it's folk ringing up. And they make out you're all friends. Everybody friends. Well we're not friends. We've got each other, and that's enough.

June But that's it. You won't always have each other.

Mam Oh, hell and damnation. Do you think we don't know that? Youth.

June I'm not youth. Don't call me youth. I wish I was youth.

Dad (*comfortingly*) You are youth.

Pause

June Can I have that scone?

Mam Go on.

June eats the scone slowly

Dad Some more tea?

He gets her it. June has got out an exercise book and is looking through it

Mam What's that?

June is on the edge of tears

June My notes. "Conduct of Interviews" ... I've gone wrong somewhere ... it's my fault ... we're in a confrontation situation now... well, you shouldn't get into a confrontation situation; Mr Farquarson says, you get into a confrontation situation you've slipped up... Cars — it's much more open and shut. It's just a case of, "Do you mind telling me your ultimate destination? Thank you. Drive on." I'm maybe not suited to people.

She blows her nose

Dad You are. I'm sure you are. You're doing champion. We're not good at interviews, probably, are we Mam?
Mam Have this other scone.

June takes it and eats it quickly

That's right.
June Transport, I was in a rut. Mr Stringfellow said, "Take this sideways jump, June, and there'll be so many more doors open to you".
Dad Listen. You did right. We've got a daughter. *She's* ambitious. "Life is for living." That's her motto.
June Well, let's have another go. (*She takes up the clipboard again*) This is Margaret, is it?
Mam Yes.
June That's question four. (*Reading again*) "The council does not aim to replace family responsibility, only to supplement it, particularly in cases where senior citizens are childless." So you're not childless. You've got a daughter. (*She writes down "Margaret"*)

Mam and Dad look at one another

Any other siblings? I didn't know that either. It means brothers and sisters. No?

Mam looks at Dad again

Dad (*firmly*) No.

June Is Margaret married?

Mam No. Are you married?

June No.

Dad She could have been married. Married three or four times over if she wanted.

Mam You'll have boyfriends?

June Oh yes. And lives where?

Dad London. Where else?

Mam She has a flat.

Dad She's a personal secretary.

June (*writing*) A secretary.

Dad No, not a secretary. A personal secretary. Her boss is to do with this ceramic heating.

June I've not heard of it.

Dad We hadn't heard of it. It's these heated pottery panels. Set in. And being pottery it retains the heat without running up lot of expenditure on electricity. I've got a lot of literature about it if you're interested.

Mam She's not interested, Dad. It's only with it being our Margaret that he's interested. Ceramic heating!

Dad She could have gone to university if she'd wanted. But she said, "Dad, I want to get on with life". So she took a secretarial course and started off at Brunskill's in Cardigan Road. It was just an ordinary job in the office, with no responsibility. But as Margaret says, "You make your own responsibility." It was old Mr Brunskill picked her out, saw she wasn't like half the girls in offices, just marking time till they find the right man. She's never been all that interested in the opposite sex, our Margaret.

Mam It was always, "What does he do? Does his work take him to faraway places?" She had a passion for geography. It was always, "Get out the atlas, Dad. Show me Perth. Rio de Janeiro." I said to her last time she was home, Did you ever dream you'd be in Valparaiso? But she's very modest, just laughed.

June I'd like to travel. I never go anywhere.

Mam Daughters, they used to live round the corner. All that's gone.

Dad She comes up to see us whenever her schedule permits. She flies to Leeds sometimes. Takes air travel in her stride. More people are killed on the roads. It's a new breed.

June When did she come up last?

Dad When did she come up, Mam? It's only a week or two since.

Mam March.

Dad As long as that? It's with speaking to her on the phone.

June Question three. (*She ticks it off*) So you're on the phone.

Dad Margaret made us have one installed so she could keep in touch.

Mam It was for her convenience. She has to have the phone when she's here anyway. Last time her boss rang up in the middle of the night wanting her to fly to Düsseldorf.

Dad She says the telephone is one of the tools of her trade. She won't be much older than you and she's on a five-figure salary.

Mam You won't be badly off, will you, love? The council, it's a good job these days. My uncle worked for the council.

Dad It's not like the private sector.

Mam You've got the satisfaction, though, haven't you? Helping people.

Dad I noticed you didn't take sugar. Margaret doesn't take sugar. She has a bit of a struggle with her figure. Has to steer clear of the carbohydrates. It's all these business lunches. She could have whatever she wanted to drink but it's generally, "May I please have an orange juice." Left on her own she'd as soon have a bit of cheese and an apple.

Mam You've got a better figure than our Margaret.

Dad Has she? I'd 've thought they were about the same. (*He gets some snaps*) This is her. Taken at Turin Airport.

Mam She dresses very simply. Crisp white blouse. A few well-chosen accessories.

Dad (*showing her a snap*) Amsterdam. She can look stunning but her aim is to blend in with the background. She says an ideal secretary should not be noticed, just taken for granted. (*Showing her another*) Los Angeles.

Mam Though she can tick people off. She put a woman in her place at Leeds and Bradford Airport. I was embarrassed. I don't know

where she gets that from. Not Dad, anyway. He never speaks up.
Have you travelled?

June Only Spain.

Mam Everybody seems to have been to Spain now. Except us.
They've been to Spain next door. They fetched us a little doll
back. It was nothing. We like Scarborough.

Dad Margaret goes all over. You'd be staggered if I told you her
itinerary. I've got to know the names of airports just from listening
to her converse. Paris: Charles de Gaulle. Chicago: O'Hare.
Rome: Fiumicino. Her boss would be lost without her.

Mam But that's all it is, purely professional. He's married with two
grown-up sons, one of them at veterinary college. Our Margaret's
like a friend of the family. She's spent Christmas with them.

Dad Only because she couldn't get up here.

June And you don't have a car?

Dad No.

Mam We could have done. We could just about have run to a car
but Dad wouldn't learn.

Dad It makes it more of a treat when Margaret comes up. Last time
she ran us out to Fountains Abbey.

June So "no car".

Mam You've got your poise back now, love, haven't you? Asking
your questions. It's just a case of having confidence.

June Thank you.

A pause, before Dad reverts to his own topic of interest

Dad She's got confidence, our Margaret. She's quite at home in
hotels. Can choose from a menu without turning a hair. And she
knows all the vintage years. But when it comes to her, as I say it's,
"Can I just have an orange juice, please."

Mam Where have your parents split up to?

June Mam's in Armley. I don't know where my dad is. I'm always
going down home.

Mam That's nice. Nice for your mam.

June Nice for us both. This old people's warden will just keep a
quiet eye on you. You won't even know he's there.

Mam It's a him, is it?

June It could be a her, either.

Dad That's the law nowadays, isn't it? Has to be a him or a her. When our Margaret was first starting there was none of that. She had to fight every inch of the way.

Mam Oh, Dad. Not fight.

Dad You don't know. We get postcards from all over. I've got booksfull. If we had grandchildren it would be a real geography lesson. Where's the one we had from Washington?

Mam Upstairs. In my drawer.

June It doesn't matter.

Mam No, let him.

Dad has gone

June is on her feet ready to go

Sit down. (*Urgently*) Sit down, love.

June sits down

We've told a lie. We have two children. We had a son. After Margaret. Colin. Only he wasn't right. He's in a home near Otley.

June That's all right. I don't need to know that. Your daughter's the one that matters.

Mam We never talk about it to anybody. We never talk about it to each other. We ought to do, only he won't.

June I won't write it down …

She is nonplussed, not really wanting to know, either, and hides her confusion by consulting her notebook

Mam We thought he was all right, only our Margaret could tell. She wouldn't play with him. Wouldn't have anything to do with him. In the finish we couldn't cope. We waited too long, I think. He was born after Dad got back from the war. We reckon to go once a month only they don't run enough buses. He knows us. We just go and sit our on a seat somewhere, weather permitting. He'd miss us if we didn't go.

June I don't know what to say. It's not to do with this, that. It's more … private.

Mam He's like a child. I look at him and think, well if he was a proper lad he'd be married now, with grown-up kiddies. Margaret won't marry. She's not the marrying sort. She's happy, that's the main thing.

June I get the impression … correct me if I'm wrong: she wouldn't come back, Margaret. I mean, say something happened … to look after you.

Mam I never said that.

June No. But … they tell us to listen to the things you're not saying. Mr Farquarson says that the things you're not saying are more important than the things you are saying.

Mam What about this other?

June I don't know.

They sit, June smiling with embarrassment. Dad is coming back

Mam Don't say I said.

June shakes her head

Dad comes in with the postcard

Dad (*sarcastically*) Your drawer! It was in the scullery. Washington.

June Nice.

Mam It'll be all cars, same as everywhere else.

Dad I've been abroad a bit myself.

Mam He was in Tunisia.

Dad Not only Tunisia. Tunisia. Libya, North Africa, Sicily. I saw Monty once. He came past in a jeep and waved. It's not many people can say that.

June One last thing. In the event of an emergency, say you're both ill, who looks after you?

Dad Well we wouldn't both be ill, would we?

June I'm trying to look ahead.

Dad We shouldn't want our Margaret coming back, would we? She's got her own life to lead.

Mam We should just have to manage.

June Supposing the worst came to the worst. There was just one of you.

Dad She'd come back. Only I wouldn't let her. I discussed it with her once. She said, "Well, Dad. We all get older. Life is for living, that's my philosophy." I don't think you should expect it of your children.

Mam I looked after my mother.

Dad You weren't a career woman.

June No close neighbours? Nobody who could come in.

Mam Next door'd come in all right, given the chance. Don't put her down.

June makes a final note and closes her file

June The only other thing is to give you this card.

She fishes in her bag for a card, one of a bunch. She gives one to Dad. He looks at it. It says "HELP!" in large red letters

It's just in case we have a winter like last year. If for some reason or other you can't get out. You pop this in the window and the warden'll know to call.

Dad *(reading the card)* "Help!" Bit stark is that, isn't it?

June It says it all, that's the point. You haven't got to be ashamed of asking for help, particularly now you're older. Everybody's getting them, the old, the disabled.

Mam *(drily)* People "at risk".

June That's right.

They are in the hall

Dad It's been a nice change for us talking to you. We don't get many visitors.

June Don't thank me. It's you that's done me the favour. Helped me with my course. Mr Farquarson says, "Sit and chat. Learn how to draw people out. Get them talking. That's your job."

June catches Mam's eye and looks away, confused. She has turned them into guinea pigs again. Dad opens the door

Dad Good luck with your chosen career.

June You too. Well, your retirement anyway.

Mam And think on, try and find yourself a man.

Dad You do what you want.

June lingers, not having mastered the art of leaving

Happiness, that's the main thing.

June Anyway ...

And on this tentative note June closes the door

They go back into the living-room. Dad sits down in the easy chair. Mam stands by the window. Pause

Dad She seemed nice enough.

Mam doesn't say anything

Mam She wants to find herself a chap.

Pause

Dad What do I do with this card, Help? What d'you think?

Mam It's telling the whole street. We'll keep it, just in case. I'll put it in my drawer.

Dad We won't let our Margaret see it. (*Pause*) Makes you feel older.

Pause

Mam More leaves coming down. Mess. (*Pause*) It never stops.

It is dusk and she begins to draw the curtains

FURNITURE AND PROPERTY LIST

On stage: Sofa
                Armchair
                Table
                Atlas
                Photographs

Off stage: Bag containing identity card, clipboard, form, pencil, note-book, exercise book, handkerchief, "HELP!" card (**June**)
                Tray with tea and plate of scones (**Mam**)
                Plastic lemon, plates (**Dad**)
                Sideplates (**Mam**)
                Postcard (**Dad**)

LIGHTING PLOT

Property fittings required: nil

Interior. The same scene throughout

To open: General interior lighting; gradual dusk effect outside window

No cues

EFFECTS PLOT

Cue 1   **Dad**: "... carpets, sugar, papermaking ..."   (Page 2)
           Doorchimes